CONTENTS

WHAT IS BODY PAINTING?	4
PAINTS AND METHODS	6
ANCIENT CIVILIZATIONS	8
CHINA AND JAPAN	10
HINDUISM AND HENNA	12
AUSTRALIA AND OCEANIA	14
AFRICA I	16
AFRICA II	18
AMERICA	20
EUROPE	22
SIGNS AND SYMBOLS	24
STAGE, FILM AND TV	26
AROUND THE WORLD	28
FURTHER INFORMATION	30
GLOSSARY	31
INDEX	32

Words appearing in bold, **like this**, are explained in the Glossary.

WHAT IS BODY PAINTING?

A universal art

In just about every culture in the world, both past and present, people have painted their bodies. The ancient Britons covered themselves with blue **woad** for battles, and the Surma people of Ethiopia paint patterns all over each other to take part in stick-fighting contests. At international matches, soccer fans paint their national flags on their faces, while **Hindu** and **Muslim** brides have their hands and feet painted with intricate patterns. Body painting is something that people from every part of the world have in common. It also unites us with our oldest **ancestors**.

How painting began

No one knows exactly how old body painting is, but experts are sure it started in **prehistoric** times, when most people lived in small groups and survived by hunting and gathering food. It could have been going on for as long as 100,000 years. In fact, body art, such as body painting, tattooing and piercing, may be the oldest kind of art in the world.

Archaeologists have found red body paint at prehistoric burial sites. This suggests body painting was used on important occasions, or as part of religious ceremonies. Experts think people may also have painted their bodies to try to give themselves magic powers.

This is a prehistoric rock painting from Argentina. It was probably made by someone filling their mouth with paint, then spitting it out in a spray to cover their hand and leaving a shape on the wall.

Body Art

BODY
PAINTING

Anna Claybourne

Heinemann
LIBRARY

www.heinemann.co.uk/library
Visit our website to find out more information about **Heinemann Library** books.

To order:
☎ Phone 44 (0) 1865 888066
▤ Send a fax to 44 (0) 1865 314091
▤ Visit the Heinemann Bookshop at www.heinemann.co.uk/library to browse our catalogue and order online.

First published in Great Britain by Heinemann Library,
Halley Court, Jordan Hill, Oxford OX2 8EJ, part of Harcourt
Education. Heinemann is a registered trademark of
Harcourt Education Ltd.

© Harcourt Education Ltd 2005
First published in paperback in 2005
The moral right of the proprietor has been asserted.

Editorial: Lucy Thunder and Helen Cannons
Design: David Poole and Kamae Design
Illustrations: Kamae Design
Picture Research: Rebecca Sodergren and Elaine Willis
Production: Edward Moore

Originated by Repro Multi-Warna
Printed and bound in China by South China Printing
Company
The paper used to print this book comes from sustainable
resources.

ISBN 0 431 17923 9 (hardback)
08 07 06 05 04
10 9 8 7 6 5 4 3 2 1

ISBN 0 431 17928 X (paperback)
09 08 07 06 05
10 9 8 7 6 5 4 3 2 1

British Library Cataloguing in Publication Data

Claybourne, Anna
Body painting. – (Body art)
391.6
A full catalogue record for this book is available from the
British Library.

Acknowledgements
The Publishers would like to thank the following for
permission to reproduce photographs: Ancient Art and
Architecture/Mary Jellife p**9 bottom**; Associated Press p**25
bottom**; Associated Press/Ian Martens p**21**; Bridgeman Art
Archive p**23 top**; Camera Press/John Hooper p**15**; Corbis
pp**8**, **11 top**, **17 top**; Corbis/Yann Arthus-Bertrand p**6**;
Corbis/Tiziana Baldizzone p**16**; Corbis/Lynn Goldsmith p**5**;
Corbis/Charles & Josette Lenars p**10**; Corbis/Fulvio Roiter
p**23 bottom**; Corbis/Hubert Stadler p**4**; Corbis/Penny
Tweedie p**14**; Hulton Archive p**20**; Kobal Collection p**22**;
Panos Pictures/Jean-Leo Dugast p**12**; Panos Pictures/Gar
Powell-Evans p**25 top**; Panos Pictures/Penny Tweedie p**7
bottom**; Popperfoto p**28**; Popperfoto.com p**19**; Rex
Features p**7 top**; Rex Features/Nigel Dickinson p**24**; Rex
Features/Brian Rasic p**17 bottom**; Rex features/Robert
Wallis p**11 bottom**; Rex Features/Reg Wilson p**26**; Rex
Features/Warner Bros/Everett p**27**; Scottish Viewpoint p**29**;
Still Pictures/Magnus Andersson p**18**; Werner Forman
Archive p**13**; Werner Forman Archive/Museo Egizio, Turin p**9
top**.

Cover photograph of a Karo man from South Ethiopia, with
a clay hair bun with feathers and his face and body
decorated with chalk, reproduced with permission of Robert
Estall Photo Library/Carol Beckwith/Angela Fisher.

The Publishers would like to thank Jenny Peck, curator at the
Pitt Rivers Museum, University of Oxford, for her assistance
in the preparation of this book.

MAKE-UP

Make-up is a kind of body painting that millions of people around the world do every day, usually on their faces. While most body painting is designed to make you look very unlike your usual self, make-up is usually meant to emphasize, enhance or disguise the features you already have in order to make you look more beautiful.

Why paint your body?

There are lots of reasons for painting ourselves. Body paint can show that you belong to a particular group, club or team. It can be used to make soldiers look extra-frightening in battle, or to give them **camouflage** that helps them hide among rocks and bushes. In many societies, people paint their faces or bodies to play a particular role, either in a festival or in a public performance. This is especially true for religious occasions. Special colours of body paint are often used to mark out the priest or holy man who has the power to perform a religious ceremony.

Body painting can also be part of a **rite of passage** – a ritual to celebrate a person reaching a particular age or stage in life. And, throughout history, people have used paint simply to make themselves look more beautiful.

Rock and pop stars sometimes use body and face painting to look shocking or to jazz up a video or stage appearance. The 1970s rock band, Kiss, has inspired other singers, such as Robbie Williams, to imitate their style of face painting. This photo shows Gene Simmons of Kiss.

PAINTS AND METHODS

Earth and ashes

The first body paint was probably made of natural **pigments** (coloured substances) such as soil, clay or ground-up minerals mixed with water. Soil comes in a range of colours including orange, yellow, grey and black. People could make more colours using minerals such as chalk, red **ochre** (a kind of iron **ore**) and blue-green malachite (copper ore). Ash and charcoal made good grey and black paint, and people could also use animal blood and juices from plants.

We can find out more about ancient body painting methods from peoples who still make body paint using pigments available in their immediate surroundings. The Dinka of Sudan, for example, make yellow paint from a mixture of ash and cow's urine. In Papua New Guinea, the Mendi people paint their faces with charcoal and white clay. The Kikuyu from Kenya combine crushed chalk with animal fat to make a white paint that sticks to the skin. These recipes show us some of the ways **prehistoric** peoples could have made their body paint.

Among the Masai people of Kenya and Tanzania, traditional white body paints are used in a festival held to mark the time when young men become elders, or senior members of their group. Hundreds of men get together and paint each other in a ritual that lasts for up to five days. The Masai traditionally make body paint from minerals or plant extracts mixed with animal fats.

This man is wearing all-over body paint designed to make him look like Spiderman. It has been applied using airbrushing techniques.

Applying paint

The simplest body painting just involves rubbing paint all over your body or face with your hands. For more detailed designs, you need some kind of brush or applicator. There is evidence that early peoples used twigs or feathers to apply dots and lines of colour. Some peoples still use these methods. For example, Masai men from Kenya and Tanzania cover themselves in white body paint and then use a stick or a tuft of grass to draw patterns in the paint.

FACT

People say that skin needs to 'breathe', but breathing only takes place through the lungs – not the skin. However, the skin is used to cool down the body through sweating. So, you can be covered in body paint if the paint is non-toxic and you take care not to get too hot.

DANGEROUS PAINT

Some body paints can be deadly. In the past, people in Japan, Egypt, England and other places used to paint their faces white with a paint made from lead, a poisonous metal. Many people became ill, and some even died, when their skin absorbed poisonous chemicals from the paint.

Professional body artists, who create complex all-over designs, use fine brushes, specially made felt-tip pens containing body paint, and even **airbrushes** and spray guns that deliver a finely controlled mist of paint. This allows them to build up layers of colour and create subtle colour blends.

Face painters at fairs and festivals draw directly on to the face using stick-shaped paints and add fine details with a brush. Make-up is applied with a range of pencils, tubes, brushes and applicators made of sponge for dabbing colour onto the skin.

An Australian Aboriginal man from the Tiwi Islands in Northern Australia carefully paints his face for a ceremonial dance.

⚠ Safety

For more information and advice on applying face and body paint, see page 30.

'Jezebel ... painted her face, and attired her head, and looked out at a window.' **The Bible**, 2 Kings 9:30, showing that women have used make-up for thousands of years

Prehistoric painters

We do not know much about what kind of body painting people did before around 10,000 years ago because there are no records. However, rock paintings from after that date show people with complex and intricate body paintings.

The first body painters we know of were Stone-age peoples who lived in Africa and Australia. One painting found in Algeria, and thought to be up to 9000 years old, shows a dancing figure painted with black and white spots and lines on her legs, arms, shoulders and stomach.

Another from Namibia, which has been dated at between 2000 and 20,000 years old, shows a figure painted white from the waist down. A rock painting from Australia, showing people covered in white stripes, is probably around 10,000 years old.

Egypt and Greece

In ancient Egypt and ancient Greece, from 6000 to 2000 years ago, body painting became more detailed, and make-up was used. Wealthy Egyptian ladies would wear it on their faces to emphasize their eyes, eyebrows and lips. They also painted their fingernails and toenails. They had make-up cases and brushes, and **archaeologists** have even found make-up mirrors made of polished copper or silver. Masks and wall paintings show that men in ancient Egypt used make-up, too.

Ancient Greek **frescoes** and vase paintings show that the Greeks had a similar make-up style, especially in Athens, ancient Greece's most powerful city. A Greek poet called Eubulus, writing in about 370 BC, wrote about Greek women with melting make-up running down their faces in the hot sun.

The patterns on the bodies of the figures in this ancient Australian Aboriginal cave painting may show the types of designs and patterns ancient peoples painted on their bodies.

AN EGYPTIAN LADY'S MAKE-UP CASE

Egyptian women stored their make-up and perfume in a special box. It could contain:

- rust-coloured lipstick and blusher made from red **ochre**
- white face paint or powder made from lead
- green eyeshadow made of ground malachite, a greenish-blue copper **ore**
- black **kohl** eyeliner made from a mineral called antimony
- eyebrow colour made of a lead ore called galenite
- nail colour made from the leaves of the **henna** plant.

This ancient Egyptian make-up box was found in the tomb of the wife of a royal architect, and is over 3000 years old.

FACT

Ancient Greek women used ash as a make-up remover. An ash paste was rubbed on the skin to scrub off the make-up, then washed away.

This ancient Egyptian painting of the goddess Isis shows the type of eye make-up ancient Egyptians wore.

Roman rituals

For upper-class Roman women, make-up was so important that they could spend several hours each morning having it applied by a team of servants. As well as painting their faces, they wore white powder on their throats and arms, as it was considered desirable to have pale skin.

In Canaan, in the area that is now Israel and Jordan, both men and women used make-up. Archaeologists have found carved stone make-up holders, and applicators with rounded tips for painting the face.

CHINA AND JAPAN

Opera art

China is one of the world's oldest civilizations. Thousands of years ago, people there painted their bodies and faces to perform ceremonial religious dances, designed to please the gods and scare away evil spirits. Over time, these ceremonies developed into a form of theatre, which is today called the Peking Opera. It has a range of stock characters, such as the dragon king, the monkey king, the white tiger and the gentle lady.

Each character in the Peking Opera is represented by a particular style and pattern of face paint. The lead female character's make-up, for example, consists of a pale pink base all over the face, with a deep red covering the lips, cheeks and both sides of the nose. Jet-black, tapering lines emphasize the eyes and eyebrows.

The white tiger character is a powerful god who can fight off evil demons. His make-up is a base of white, with lines of black, pink and gold around the eyes, mouth and nose. Different colours have different meanings: red, for instance, always stands for honesty and respectability.

Painting methods

Peking Opera performers mix oil or egg-white into their paints to make their painted faces look shiny when they are on stage. There are several traditional methods of applying the paint. The hardest is called the 'hook' method. The paintbrush is held still, and the actor has to move his or her face so that the lines are drawn in exactly the right places.

Traditionally, men had to play female roles in Peking Opera, because it was seen as unsuitable for men and women to perform on stage together. The heavy, **stylized** make-up helped male actors to make themselves look convincingly female.

Singers in the Peking Opera wear traditional face paint.

Geisha style

The fashion for pale or white face paint, which crops up in many different cultures and historical periods, spread from China to Japan in around AD 600. It gradually developed into the stylized make-up worn by geishas. A geisha is a kind of specially trained female entertainer, skilled in the arts of music, conversation and serving food and tea. There are not many geishas nowadays, but in the past they were often employed at gatherings and parties.

Geishas have to move and speak according to a set of strict rules, and they must also have a perfect appearance. Geisha make-up is white, with small red lips painted in the middle of the real lips, and red and black lines above the eyes. Sometimes geishas also wear body paint on their necks, shoulders and backs. The geisha look covers up imperfections and differences between people, making all geishas look very similar to each other.

A Japanese woman wearing full geisha make-up and costume.

OUT OF THE SUN

White make-up like a geisha's has been popular throughout history. One reason for this was that having pale skin meant you had stayed out of the sun, and were therefore a wealthy **aristocrat** rather than someone who had to work outdoors. Looking tanned only became desirable among white people in the 20th century.

TODAY'S TRENDS

Elements of the geisha style can often be seen in make-up worn in modern Japan and around the world. Many women use **foundation** to make their faces appear as smooth and uniformly coloured as possible, then they use lipstick to make their lips appear extra bright and strong.

HINDUISM AND HENNA

Forehead marks

Hinduism is the main religion of India, and is practised in many other countries across the world including the UK. Hinduism plays a large part in **multicultural** societies, such as those found in Canada, the UK and the Caribbean.

According to Hindu beliefs, the forehead is one of the cleanest and purest parts of the body, because it has no features, hair or **orifices** (such as nostrils or ear holes), like those found on the rest of the face. Many women wear a red, black or gold mark on their foreheads every day. It can be a sign of religious purity and good fortune, or simply a decoration. Or, in some places, the type of dot a woman wears shows whether she is married or not.

Men wear much more complicated forehead paintings, especially for religious festivals and ceremonies. For example, if you are at a Hindu festival and you see a man with three horizontal white bands painted across his forehead, and a red dot in the middle, it means he is a follower of Shiva, the creator and destroyer, one of Hinduism's many gods. Followers of Vishnu, the god of protection and mercy, wear vertical forehead stripes instead. Hindu holy men called **sadhus** often paint themselves white or yellow from head to toe, or cover themselves in a layer of mud, when they go on **pilgrimages**.

For some ceremonies, children are dressed up to look like Hindu gods, who are often shown with blue skin in Hindu holy books. So the children are painted blue all over, usually with special patterns on their foreheads, too. Hindus believe it brings them good luck to give gifts and money to children who are dressed as gods.

Hands and feet

Mehndi is the Indian word for the **henna** plant, whose leaves and stalks can stain the skin and hair red. For centuries, it has been a tradition in India to paint *mehndi* patterns on women's hands and feet for weddings. As well as the bride, the female guests can have their hands and feet painted. The patterns are intricate, made up of swirling lines, dots, geometric shapes or tiny leaves and flowers. They are drawn onto the skin using a tube or bag with a narrow nozzle, filled with henna paste. When it dries and is rubbed off, the pattern is left behind as a stain.

A Hindu holy man, wearing forehead paint that shows he is a follower of the god Vishnu. It consists of a U-shaped white line with a red area in the middle. The red area represents Vishnu's wife, Lakshmi.

'This blue-necked, red-complexioned one, who traverses through the sky.' Description of the god Shiva from the Vedas, Hindu holy texts

A woman applies mehndi *paste to a friend's hands, using a bag that narrows to a tiny hole. This allows her to draw fine lines and patterns with the paste.*

According to legend, *mehndi* designs were magical and ensured good luck. They are still thought to bring good luck to a wedding, and are seen as a vital part of wedding beauty preparations. Today, some women wear *mehndi* on their arms, backs and navels as well as on their hands and feet.

HENNA AND FASHION

Henna has also been adopted by the world of fashion. You can buy tubes of henna paste for *mehndi* painting at accessory stores and make-up counters. Among the many people who have embraced henna painting is Madonna, who wore *mehndi* designs in her video for the song 'Frozen'.

Henna around the world

Henna painting is popular among **Muslims** as well as Hindus and is practised in many parts of the Middle East and North Africa. As well as looking good, it is often used as a charm to bring good luck or ward off evil spirits.

Among the Hausa people of Nigeria, the bride and groom both have their hands and arms coloured with henna, which they call *lalle*. Instead of being painted with patterns, the skin is dyed red all over. Old women paint the young couple's arms with henna paste, then wrap them and fit hollow, dried-out gourds (a type of vegetable) over them. It then takes a few days for the red colour to develop.

AUSTRALIA AND OCEANIA

Australian Aborigines

'Aborigines' is a name given to the native peoples of Australia. They have lived in Australia for 40,000 years or more, and some of them still use body-painting techniques developed thousands of years ago. Among the Aborigines, body painting can have many different meanings, depending on the occasion.

Meanings

In the past, Aborigines used paints they could make from earth, chalk and soot, so the most common colours were black, white, red and yellow. These four colours stood for the 'four elements' – earth, air, water and fire. The colours have other meanings, too. For example, red can stand for blood, and white can stand for **ancestors** who have died. In Aboriginal culture, ancestors are sacred, so a dancer might wear white body paint for a dance to celebrate or communicate with the ancestors.

At other ceremonies, Aborigines wear body paint that imitates particular animals. Alternatively they might wear **geometric** patterns that show which village or **clan** they belong to.

FACT

In the 18th and 19th centuries, Christian missionaries in Australia and Oceania often tried to stop body painting because they thought it was ungodly.

These Aborigine boys in Australia are wearing body paint for a **rite of passage**, celebrating their journey from childhood into adulthood. The white patterns on their bodies show which group they belong to, and are also meant to connect their **souls** with the souls of their ancestors.

Men from the Asaro River region of Papua New Guinea wearing mud masks and body paint.

Papua New Guinea

Papua New Guinea is one of the countries that make up Oceania, the huge group of islands to the north and east of Australia. Hundreds of different peoples live in Papua New Guinea, and a lot of them are famous for their elaborate body art, which is used in many different ways.

At Huli festivals and celebrations, men wear body paint patterns that stand for their age and their position in society. Samo doctors wear paint that imitates the insides of the body, to show their role as healers. Among the Andaman islanders, family members paint themselves with matching patterns to show their relationship to each other.

In some places, it is not the colours and patterns that are important, but the glossy sheen paint gives to the skin. When a Wahgi woman gets married, for example, she wears shiny paint on her face, because glossy skin is thought to encourage ancestors to grant people good fortune.

The Mendi people use body painting to predict the future. A young woman has her face painted black and red for a traditional dance, and the way the colours blur or run during the dancing is said to reveal the fortunes that will befall the village.

Painted with clay

The people of the Asaro River region in Papua New Guinea are famous for their rituals involving clay from their local mudbanks. According to legend, many years ago their village was attacked, and the warriors went and hid on the muddy riverbank. When they returned, caked in clay from head to toe, their enemies thought they were evil spirits and fled in terror. Today the people of Asaro still celebrate this victory by wearing clay masks and painting their bodies with clay.

'We are born beautiful. But we also have the power to enhance that beauty.' **A Wodaabe** bridegroom

African traditions

The huge continent of Africa is home to hundreds of different peoples. As well as being divided into countries, such as Nigeria, Sudan and Kenya, Africa has many **ethnic groups**, such as the Yoruba, the San, the Surma and the Nuba. These peoples lived in old kingdoms across Africa before the continent was divided up into today's countries. So, for example, the Masai people once dominated much of East Africa. Today they live in Tanzania and Kenya, but still keep their **identity** as a group. Many ethnic groups like these have their own body art ceremonies and customs which have been preserved over thousands of years.

In countries such as Algeria in North Africa, where people have quite pale skin, tattooing is more popular than body painting. In countries like Cameroon and Kenya – south of the Sahara Desert – most people have darker skin that tattoos do not show up on. So body painting, especially with white and bright colours like red and yellow, is an important part of traditional ceremonies and rituals.

Wodaabe beauty contests

The Wodaabe people from Niger are **nomadic**, which means they travel from place to place with their herds of animals. Once a year, they meet up for a huge, week-long gathering called the Geerewol. It is a chance for young people to meet each other and for marriages to be set up. To encourage this, the Wodaabe hold a 'Bridegrooms' Parade'. The young men have to dance and pull faces to impress the girls, who get to choose the boys they like best.

To look his best for the parade, each boy must paint his face to make himself look as beautiful as possible. During the Geerewol the young men carry plastic **cosmetic** mirrors so they can constantly check their appearance and reapply their make-up.

This Wodaabe bridegroom has painted most of his face yellow, and emphasized the length of his nose with a narrow red line. The face he is making is part of the dance. He is making himself even more attractive to the women by showing off the whites of his eyes and his white teeth.

This Surma woman is wearing face and body paint for the donga.

Surma stick fights

The Surma people live mostly in Ethiopia, in Eastern Africa. Several times a year, Surma from different villages get together for donga, or stick fights, between the young men. The fights are not meant to be dangerous, but like the Wodaabe Bridegroom's Parade, they give the men a chance to show off and impress the young women.

Before the fights, the men paint each other all over with white patterns. First the face and body are covered with a white paint made of water and chalk, and then swirls, lines and spirals are made with the fingers while the paint is still wet. The idea behind the paint patterns is to look so frightening and impressive that you scare your opponent before the fighting even begins. The paint also acts as a mark of identification, since each village uses its own arrangement of patterns.

Surma women also wear body paint for the donga, although they are just there to watch. They use a wider range of shapes and colours, including stripes and leaf-shapes painted in white and filled in with bright red.

WODAABE MAKE-UP

These are the main features of a Wodaabe bridegroom's make-up:
- cheeks painted white or yellow
- darker shading around the jaw to make the face look thinner
- a long white, yellow or red stripe down the centre of the face to lengthen the nose
- black make-up around the eyes and mouth to emphasize the whiteness of eyeballs and teeth
- extra dots, spirals, stars, flowers or other designs for decoration.

MAKE-UP FOR MEN

Around the world, women are more likely to wear make-up than men. However, as the Wodaabe bridegrooms show, make-up can be just as important for men as for women. Ancient Greek and ancient Egyptian men often wore it and today it is especially popular among male pop stars and celebrities. Examples include the singers Michael Jackson and David Bowie, and the comedian Eddie Izzard. The pop star Marilyn Manson, shown here, often wears full face make-up.

The amazing Nuba

The Nuba people, who live in Sudan, are among the most famous body artists in the world. For them, body painting is a mark of youth, strength and attractiveness. Nuba boys and young men between the ages of about 10 and 30 are the most likely to paint themselves, but girls sometimes wear body paint, too.

Each Nuba man is responsible for painting his own face and body with his own designs. He must put a lot of effort into making his designs as creative and beautiful as possible, as his reputation and popularity will depend on his painting skills. But there are many rules and restrictions.

Firstly, each clan has its own colours and styles and these must be stuck to. Secondly, men can only use certain colours once they reach a certain age. Young boys may only use red and white. When they officially become young men, they may use yellow, and only the older men are allowed to use black. If a boy uses colours he is not allowed to, he may be punished by the elders of his village.

The ritual of doing the painting is important, too. Before applying the paint, a Nuba man must wash, shave off all his body hair, and cover himself in oil. The paint, usually made from coloured minerals, is applied with the fingers, sticks or brushes made from tufts of straw. The Nuba also carve wooden stamps which can be dipped in paint and used to make a repeated pattern on the skin.

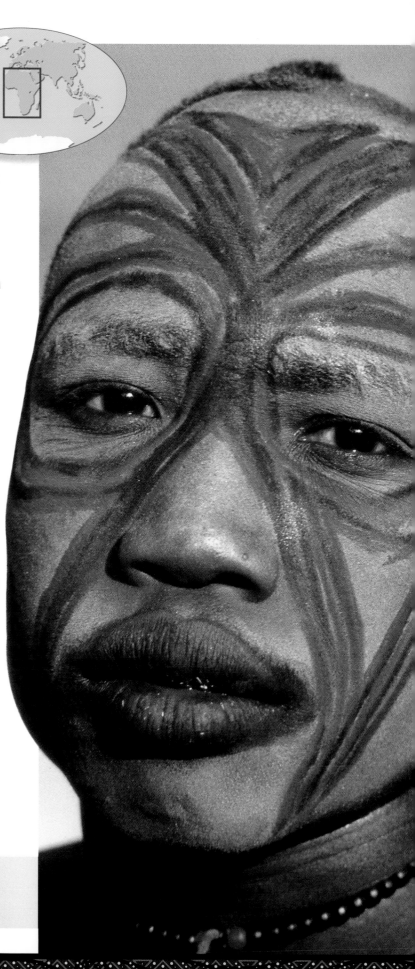

A Nuba man from Sudan wears a pattern of red, black and white paint on his face.

Mangbetu markings

The Mangbetu people are from the region that is now Zaire. In the past, they created very elaborate body paintings, made up of fine red or black lines arranged in complex patterns and shapes. These acted as **status** symbols. If you wore a complete set of lines, it showed you had the time and money to have your body painted by skilled servants. The Mangbetu language is still used, but their kingdom does not exist any more.

Uli painting

Uli painting is practised by the Igbo people of Nigeria, though much less today than in the past. Traditionally, Igbo women wore uli paint to show that they were ready for marriage. It is designed to show off the parts of the body, such as the neck and legs, which the Igbo consider to be the most beautiful.

To prepare for uli painting, the skin is shaved to remove any hair, and then covered in a bright red powder. Lines are then drawn on top using a dye made from the seeds of uli plants. The dye turns black or dark blue overnight, making a striking pattern which lasts for up to eight days.

These Nuba dancers have white streaks across their arms and legs. For the Nuba people, body painting is a mark of youth, strength and attractiveness.

FACT

Queen Mutubani of the Mangbetu, who ruled in the early 20th century, had three serving girls to paint her body with lines, but it still took several hours.

AMERICA

American peoples

Native Americans are the people who lived in the Americas before outsiders, such as Europeans, first went there. Today, Native American peoples such as the Tlingit, the Sioux and the Maya still live in the USA, Canada and Central and South America.

Body painting is an extremely important part of Native American culture, especially for those groups from the west of North America, such as the Cree, the Pomeiok and the Pamlico. In the past, they painted their bodies so extensively that some of the explorers who met them thought they were fully clothed, when in fact they were wearing mainly body paint. However, Native Americans do not practise body art as much today as they used to hundreds of years ago.

Ceremonial dances

Peoples like the Cherokee and the Sioux did special dances to mark the seasons, to celebrate a victory, or to summon (call up) a particular type of weather – the rain dance is the most famous example. It was extremely important to paint the body for these occasions. Within each group, different colours were given different meanings. For the Cherokee, for example, red **symbolized** victory in battle, white meant peace and joy, and black stood for death.

Important individuals, such as chiefs, used to paint their faces in patterns and colours that showed their past achievements and their **status**. The men also put on 'war paint' to make themselves look frightening for battles.

This is a 19th-century painting of Little White Bear, a member of a Native American group known as the Kaw or Konza. It clearly shows his red body and face paint.

This Native American girl dances at a pow-wow held in Alberta, Canada in 2002. She is wearing traditional dress and face paint.

FACT

European explorers sometimes called Native Americans 'redskins', probably because of their use of red body paint.

In the rainforest

Central and South America are home to hundreds of different **Amerindian** peoples, including rainforest-dwellers such as the Yanomami and the Kayapo. Like many peoples around the world, the Kayapo honour and respect their **ancestors**. At their Kwarup ceremony, wooden posts are used to represent dead members of their **ethnic group**. The posts and the people are painted in the same patterns – circles, stripes and triangles in black, red and white – to link the **souls** of the living and the dead. At the end of the ceremony, the souls of the dead are set free to live in the spirit world.

Red pigments

The Illinois people often painted their bodies with a red colour called **ochre**. They obtained this from oxidised iron deposits (similar to rust) that they found in the ground. Later, around 1700, they started to use vermilion, another red pigment. They got this by trading with the French. Women and children painted their cheeks with red paint, and the men often covered their whole faces with red and black paint. The Yanomami people use annatto, a spice, to make a red paint, which they use along with black paint to decorate their bodies.

'An unpainted body is a stupid body.' **Saying of the Cadureo people** of Brazil

EUROPE

Woad-wearers

When you think of body painting in Europe, you probably think of face-painters at festivals, or modern stage and TV make-up. But European body-painting has a long history. As long ago as 55 BC, and probably before, ancient British warriors painted themselves blue to make themselves look scary in battle. They were trying to fight off the Romans, who were taking Britain over at that time.

The blue colouring they used came from **woad**, a kind of plant. As well as making the warriors look strange and wild, experts think the act of putting on the paint probably helped them to prepare themselves for battle. As in many other cultures, applying body paint was an important ritual in itself which helped people to see themselves as belonging to a group or team.

The film Braveheart *featured actors dressed as Scottish warriors charging into battle. They were painted blue to look as if they were wearing woad.*

Make-up and beauty

The period from the 16th to the 18th century in Europe was a great age for make-up. It was fashionable to have very pale skin, so women painted their faces, necks and chests with bright white make-up that contained lead. However, the lead was so poisonous that women regularly died from using it – in those days people did not realize that lead was so deadly.

FACT

The Picts, an ancient Scottish tribe who painted themselves before battles, get their name from the Latin word *picti*, which means 'painted ones'.

'All the Britons, indeed, dye themselves with woad, which occasions a bluish colour, and thereby have a more terrible appearance in fight.'
Julius Caesar, a great Roman soldier and leader who lived from c.100–44 BC

This painting of Queen Elizabeth I of England shows the white-faced appearance that was fashionable during her reign in the 16th and early 17th centuries.

Carnival!

As in many other cultures around the world, Europeans often wear body paint for festivals and celebrations. At the Venice carnival in Italy, partygoers wear white masks or paint their faces white. At the Notting Hill Carnival in London, dancers combine body paint with huge, elaborate costumes made of brightly coloured foil, feathers and fabric.

This festival-goer in Venice, Italy, is wearing white face paint as part of his costume.

Women also emphasized their cheeks and lips with **rouge**, made from wax mixed with **cochineal** (a red **pigment** taken from a type of insect). Some women also drew in fake eyebrows, spread egg white on their face to make their skin look shiny and stiff and drew blue veins onto their skin to make it look even whiter. And they used **kohl** eye make-up, made from powdered antimony (a mineral) just like the ancient Egyptians did.

Although it was more popular among women, men also wore the white-faced look, especially in France. At the time of the French Revolution in 1789, most French society gentlemen wore white face powder, red lipstick and rouge on their cheeks.

SIGNS AND SYMBOLS

Standing for something

Body painting is sometimes done for purely **aesthetic** reasons – that is, because it looks good. Just as often, the colours and designs used in body painting are **symbolic**, which means they stand for something. For example, they can symbolize someone's membership of a group, their past achievements or their position in the society they live in. Or people can be painted to represent a god or spirit, or a type of animal.

Animal art

In many body-painting traditions around the world, people paint themselves to look like animals. There are lots of reasons for this. People might want to worship an animal god, try to gain an animal's qualities, drive away pests or make a hunt more successful.

Face painters at fairs and festivals often paint people's faces to look like animals. These children are wearing leopard and tiger face paint.

Mehinaku and Waura people from South America paint themselves with spots to symbolize the jaguar. This is thought to help the wearer take on some of the jaguar's power and cunning. Traditional Australian Aboriginal animal dances and body art are meant to win the support and help of animal spirits, such as the Rainbow Serpent.

Skeletons

Peoples from all over the world use body paint to draw bones and skulls on their skin. This is probably because of the human need to make sense of what happens when we die.

Ancient Australian Aboriginal rock paintings, which experts know as 'X-ray' paintings, show people with their bones and internal organs showing. Lobi girls from Burkina Faso in Africa wear white skeleton body paint to symbolize their **ancestors**, who are thought to come back to life in the form of young women. Many other African groups also wear skeleton patterns for ancestor-worshipping ceremonies.

In Mexico, people remember their dead relatives on the Day of the Dead, in early November, by dressing up as skeletons with their faces painted as skulls. In Europe and America, this festival takes the form of Hallowe'en, a couple of days earlier. Today, children often celebrate Hallowe'en by wearing any kind of fancy dress. They often use face paints to disguise themselves as skeletons, witches or ghosts.

A woman taking part in a Day of the Dead parade in Los Angeles, USA, wearing skull face paint.

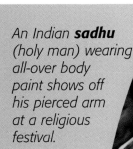

*An Indian **sadhu** (holy man) wearing all-over body paint shows off his pierced arm at a religious festival.*

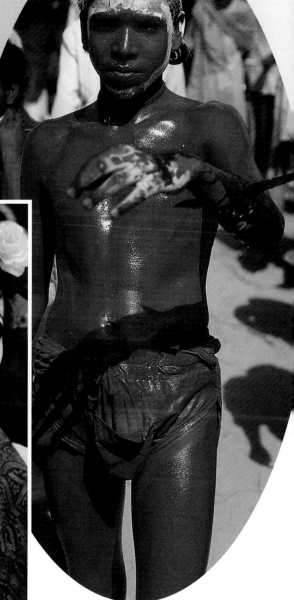

STAGE, FILM AND TV

Performance art

In the first theatres, in ancient Greece, actors wore masks with exaggerated facial expressions on them, so that even the people right at the back could see them. Stage make-up serves the same purpose. It emphasizes the features, making an actor's face easy to see even from the very back of a large theatre.

Stage make-up is also used for special effects. Actors can make their skin greyer and add wrinkles to make themselves look much older than they are, or paint hollows under their eyes to make them look tired and ill. Men can even have paint applied to their bodies to give the effect of a hairy or muscly chest.

Actors have also used face and body make-up to help them play a member of the opposite sex. In Shakespeare's day, as in many theatrical traditions around the world, only male actors performed on the stage, so they needed lots of make-up to play female parts. Also, in the past, white actors like Laurence Olivier used to 'black up', or put on dark make-up, to play the part of Shakespeare's famous black character Othello. Today, the part is much more likely to go to a black actor.

Pantomime is one form of theatre in which actors still wear huge amounts of make-up and paint. This male actor is wearing exaggerated female make-up to play a pantomime dame.

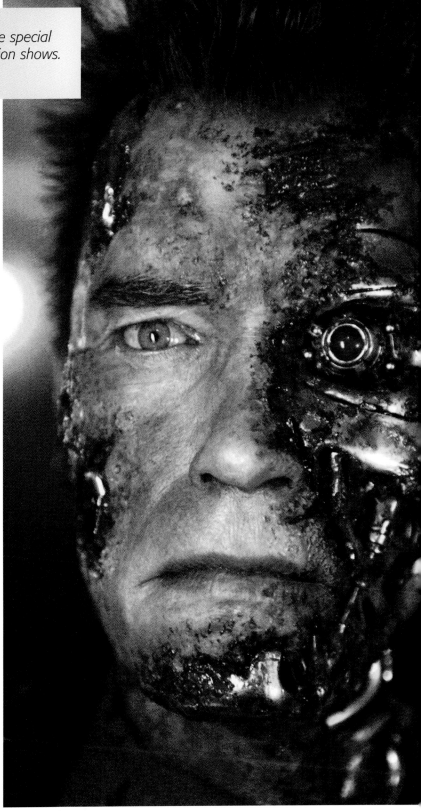

Skilled make-up artists and body painting artists create special effects, such as this android face, for films and television shows. This is Arnold Schwarzenegger in Terminator 3.

On the screen

When film was invented in the 1890s, make-up was still vital. The first films were silent and black-and-white, and strong make-up helped to distinguish different characters.

Even though film shows faces clearly, and we do not need make-up to help us see the actors' expressions, almost everyone – both male and female – who appears in a film or on TV today is wearing lots of make-up. The bright lights used for filming can make natural skin look washed-out, and close-ups reveal marks, like spots and wrinkles, which make-up is used to hide.

Body colour

All-over body painting is becoming more and more popular in film and TV. It is used in pop videos, films, TV advertisements and billboards. This is partly because a person painted, for example, gold, silver or green all over is instantly attention-grabbing, giving a video or advert an advantage over the competition.

On the *Star Trek* TV programmes and films, body paint is used to give different patterns and markings to characters from different parts of the galaxy. This body and face paint can take several hours to apply each time.

DISEASES AND INJURIES

A special kind of body art is required to recreate injuries for medical TV dramas such as *ER*. A skilled make-up artist can create realistic-looking cuts, bruises and skin diseases. Special make-up is also used to make living actors look like dead bodies for the screen.

FACT

Circus clowns each design their own unique make-up style. It is considered bad manners to copy another clown's face.

Showing support

Body painting still has many of the same functions in modern life as it has had for thousands of years: marking special occasions, making you more attractive, and showing which group you belong to.

Using face paint to show **allegiance** happens most often at sporting events. Like the Surma preparing for their stick fights (see page 17), soccer, tennis and cricket fans paint themselves to show which team they are supporting. The most popular option is to wear your country's flag painted all over your face, but some supporters paint their country's colours on their bodies, too.

Painting styles can also show you belong to a particular cultural group, or like a certain kind of music. Punk and goth styles are good examples – they both developed in Europe, the USA and Australia in the late 20th century. Punk make-up involves strong or bright colours, often painted around the eyes or on the cheeks in complex designs. Goth style sometimes involves a plain white face with black eye colour and black, dark red or purple lips.

A Scottish soccer fan wears the Scottish flag painted on his face at an England–Scotland match.

MODERN MAKE-UP

Even when they are not celebrating, dressing up or supporting their team, millions of people around the world wear body paint every single day in the form of facial **cosmetics**. You might not think that is proper body painting, but a European woman's **foundation**, blusher, mascara and pink lipstick might seem as odd to a Wodaabe man as his yellow face, nose stripe and black lip colour seem to her. Many women feel they cannot even leave their homes without their faces completely covered in make-up – and they spend billions of pounds on make-up every year.

Festivals, fêtes and fun

Face and body painting are a growing part of all kinds of festivals and celebrations. Children can have their faces painted at almost any kind of fair or fête, and adults wear face paint for fancy dress parties and carnivals. Even though most people no longer organize their lives around body-painting ceremonies, it seems to be a natural part of being human to want to dress up and disguise ourselves with paint.

In Edinburgh in Scotland, for example, people hold celebrations based on the ancient **Celtic** tradition of **Beltane**. On 1 May every year, members of the Beltane society act out **symbolic** dances and parades, using body paint to help them play the parts of red men, white women and the **Green Man**. Detailed, highly artistic body painting has become a branch of the fine art world. Expert body painters train for years to perfect their craft, and perform complicated body paintings at body art conferences and conventions.

A performer dances at the Beltane festival in Edinburgh. According to the ancient Celtic tradition, people paint themselves red to represent mischief, chaos and destructiveness. They are counteracted by the Green Man, who stands for rebirth and renewal.

FACT

Modern make-up can contain whale fat, lard, crushed insects, snails or fish scales!

Here are some more ways that body painting crops up in everyday life:

- cricketers and skiers who need to keep the sun off their faces wear their sunblock in fun colours and patterns
- you might have your hand stamped with a picture or number when you go into a club or festival, to show you have paid
- in some countries, voters at elections have their hands dipped in ink after voting, so they will be spotted if they try to go back and vote again.

Safety tips

! Putting unfamiliar substances on your skin can sometimes cause an allergic reaction. Only use paints designed for the face or body, not other paints such as wall paint or oil paint, or any other inks or dyes.

! Before you start, apply a small amount of paint to the skin and wait at least a few minutes to make sure the skin is not allergic.

! When applying face paints, take extra care not to get any in your eyes. If you do, rinse the eye with cool water.

! If you or someone else starts to get any rash, itchiness or swelling of the skin, or feels ill, wash all the paint off as soon as possible.

! If you want to try *mehndi* painting, check the henna paste has few additives.

Where to buy body paint

Some cities have special theatrical make-up stores that sell every kind of body paint. If you cannot find one, you may be able to get face paint at toyshops and supermarkets, especially at certain times of year such as Hallowe'en. You may also be able to buy body paint on the Web, and some books and websites show you how to make your own safe body paints.

Books

Decorated Skin, Karl Groning (Thames and Hudson, 1997)

Mehndi: the Art of Henna Body Painting, Carine Fabius (Random House, 1998)

The Usborne Book of Face Painting, C. Caudron and C. Childs (Usborne Publishing)

Websites

http://www.face-painter.com/HOMEPAGE.html

Faces for Kids – lots of face-painting designs to give you ideas.

http://www.mehron.com/retail/clown.cfm

Clowning Colour Application Instructions – how to create different clown faces.

http://www.museum.upenn.edu/new/exhibits/ online_exhibits/body_modification/ bodmodpaint.shtml

University of Pennsylvania Museum of Archaeology and Anthropology's 'Bodies of Cultures' online body painting exhibit 2002.

Places to visit

These museums have exhibitions where you can see different kinds of body painting from around the world. So may other regional museums – check your local newspaper for listings, or look in the national listing pages of daily newspapers, which often have this information on Saturdays.

Pitt Rivers Museum
Parks Road, Oxford, England, UK
http://www.prm.ox.ac.uk

Australian Museum
6 College Street Sydney, NSW 2010, Australia
http://www.amonline.net.au

Glossary

aesthetic   to do with beauty rather than meaning

airbrush   device used to apply paint in the form of a fine spray

allegiance   loyalty to a particular group or team

allergic reaction   rash, swelling, sneezing or other problem caused by the body reacting against a normally harmless substance such as metal or dust

Amerindian   people descended from those who lived in South America before Europeans arrived there

ancestor   family member who lived a long time ago

archaeologists   people who find out about the past by studying the remains of old human settlements

aristocrat   member of the ruling classes

Beltane   ancient Celtic festival held to mark the arrival of spring

camouflage   colours and patterns that blend in with the surroundings to provide a disguise

Celtic   to do with a group of peoples, called Celts, who lived in various parts of Europe over 2000 years ago

clan   group of people linked by family ties

cochineal   red colouring made from the dried and powdered bodies of a type of insect

cosmetic   decorative or to do with appearances. "Cosmetics" is another word for make-up.

ethnic group   group of people who share things such as language, culture or religion

foundation   type of make-up worn all over the face to give it a smooth, flat colour

fresco   painting on a plaster wall

geometric   to do with mathematical shapes, such as triangles and rectangles

Green Man   traditional symbolic figure found in many cultures around the world. He represents spring, growth and fertility.

henna   plant that releases a red pigment from its leaves and stalks

Hinduism   religion popular in India and South-east Asia

identity   person's sense of who they are and what culture they belong to

indigenous   belonging to a place. For example, the Australian Aboriginal people are indigenous to Australia.

kohl   type of black eye-make-up, originally made from a metal called antimony

mehndi   Indian word for henna, and also for patterns painted on the hands and feet using henna paste

missionaries   members of a religion, especially Christianity, who travel to other countries to try to spread their religious beliefs to others

multicultural   containing many different peoples and cultures

Muslim   follower of Islam, one of the world's biggest religions

Native Americans   peoples who lived in North America before explorers from Europe arrived there

nomadic   moving from place to place, for example to follow herds of animals or to do seasonal work

ochre   type of earth that contains a lot of iron. It can be yellow, orange or brownish-red.

ore   substance that contains a useful mineral. For example, malachite is a copper ore and contains copper.

orifice   hole in the body, such as the mouth or ear hole

pigment   another name for a colour or dye

pilgrimage   journey to a religious shrine or holy place

prehistoric   the time up to about 10,000 years ago, before history started to be written down

rite of passage   ceremony held to celebrate reaching a certain age or stage of life

rouge   make-up used for making the cheeks look red. Also called blusher.

sadhu   holy man who lives a life of meditation or self-deprivation

soul   person's mind or spirit, the part of them that is not their body. Many people believe the soul lives on after the body dies.

status   standing or level of respect that a person has in their society

stylized   created according to a particular style, rather than looking exactly realistic

symbol/symbolic/symbolize   a symbol stands for, or symbolizes, an idea – for example, an ear piercing could be a symbol of wealth. If something acts as a symbol, it is said to be symbolic.

woad   type of plant which produces a blue dye, which is also called woad

INDEX

Africa 6, 7, 8, 13, 16–19, 25
airbrushing 7
allegiance 5, 14, 24, 28
allergic reactions 30
Americas 20–1, 25
Amerindian peoples 21
ancestor worship 14, 21, 25
animal art 24–5
Australian Aborigines 14, 25
Aztecs 5

beauty parades 16
Beltane 29
body painting
    allergic reactions 30
    ancient civilizations 4, 5, 8–9
    in everyday life 29
    methods 6–7, 10, 12, 13, 17,
        18, 19
    reasons for 5, 24
    safety 7, 30
bridegrooms 16, 17
brides 4, 12–13
Britons 4, 22
Burkina Faso 25

camouflage 5
celebrities 5, 13, 17
ceremonial dances 14, 20, 21, 29
China 10
clay painting 15
clowns 27

Day of the Dead 25
Dinka people 6
donga (stick fights) 4, 17

Egypt 7, 8, 9
Ethiopia 4, 17
European body painting 7,
    22–3, 25

face painters 7, 22, 24, 29
festivals 5, 6, 7, 12, 15, 23, 24, 29
film and TV make-up 27
forehead marks 12
foundation 11, 28

geisha make-up 11
Greece 8, 9, 26
Guinea 19

Hallowe'en 25
Hausa people 13
henna 9, 12, 13, 30
Hinduism 4, 12

Igbo people 19

Japan 7, 11

Kayapo people 21
Kenya 6, 7, 16
kohl 9, 23

lead paints 7, 22
Loma people 19

magic powers 4, 13, 25
make-up 5, 7, 8, 9, 10, 11, 16, 17,
    22, 23, 26–7, 28, 29
make-up remover 9
Mangbetu people 19
Masai people 6, 7, 16
medical dramas 27
mehndi painting 12–13, 30
Mexico 25
Muslims 4, 13

Native Americans 20, 21
Nigeria 13, 19
nomadic peoples 16
non-toxic paints 7
Nuba people 18

ochre 6, 9, 21, 25

paints 6, 7, 10, 12, 14, 15, 19, 21,
    22, 23
pale skin 9, 11, 22, 23
pantomime 26
Papua New Guinea 6, 15
Peking Opera 10
Picts 22
pigments 6, 14, 15, 21, 23
pow-wows 21
prehistoric peoples 4, 6, 8
punk and goth styles 28

red body paint 4, 25
religious beliefs 4, 5, 10, 12, 21
rites of passage 5, 6, 14, 19
rituals 16, 18, 22
rock paintings 4, 8, 25
Romans 9
rouge 23

sadhus 12, 25
safety 7, 30
skeleton body painting 25
sporting events 4, 28
stage make-up 10, 26, 30
status 15, 19, 20
stockings, painted 23
Sudan 6, 18
Surma people 4, 17, 28
symbolism 14, 24, 25, 29

tattooing 4, 16

uli painting 19

woad 4, 22
Wodaabe people 16

Zaire 19